LAND ⇒
⇐ROVER

LAND ROVER

Chris Bennett

OSPREY
AUTOMOTIVE

About the Author

Land Rover is the third book that Chris Bennett has produced for Osprey. His first two works featured military aviation subjects, the United States Air Force F-15 Eagle base at Bitburg and the Canadian Armed Forces F-18 Hornet base at Baden Söllingen, both in Germany. He has recently completed a book on the Lamborghini Countach and is currently working on a Grand Prix Volume.

All images reproduced in this book were taken with the superb Nikon F4 and F801 cameras, fitted with Nikkor lenses and loaded with Kodak Kodachrome and Fuji Velvia film stocks.

Acknowledgements

The author would like to express his grateful thanks to Land Rover Ltd who, on more than one occasion entrusted examples of their precious demonstration vehicles into his (as then) untrained and inexperienced hands. During expeditions to the beautiful but potentially hazardous green lanes of Wales whilst under the expert guidance of David Bowyer, these vehicles proved to the author first-hand the slogan 'the best four by four by far' is entirely justified and appropriate. Cheers Colin and Zak, thanks for the experience.

I offer my sincere thanks to all those who made this book possible, especially Colin Walkey, Roger Crathorne, Don Green BEM, John Carter, Josephina 'Zac' Zacaroli-Walker and Vince Hammersly of Land Rover Ltd, Nick Horne, Iain Chapman and David Arthur of R J Reynolds Int. (Camel Trophy), Tony Jardine of Jardine PR Ltd, Major Benjamin Hervey-Bathurst, Brian, Philip and Chris Bashall, Bob and Joe Ives, Dennis 'The Menace' Baldry and Shaun Barrington of Osprey, John Slator of Molinare Ltd. and technical contributor Kevan Chippindall-Higgin. Special thanks to my good friends, John Pitchforth of Nikon UK Ltd and Paul Waller of Commercial Cameras in Woking, Surrey.

For a catalogue of all books published by Osprey Automotive please write to:

The Marketing Department, Osprey Publishing, 2nd Floor, Unit 6, Spring Gardens, Tinworth Street, London SE11 5EH

Title page

When not shrouded in light reducing fog these highland areas of Wales offer some of the most picturesque scenery within the British Isles, in many instances accessible only by use of the 4 × 4

Half-title page

David Roffey runs into problems in his ex-Royal Navy lightweight on the slippery surface and gets a tug, via a kinetic recovery rope. Designed around an 88-in chassis the military $\frac{1}{2}$-ton lightweight's slab-sided appearance resulted from the weight-saving process of eliminating 'unnecessary' body panels for ease of air-portability. The $\frac{1}{2}$-ton designation refers to total load capacity

First publishd in 1992 by Osprey, an imprint of Reed Consumer Books Limited Michelin House, 81 Fulham Road London SW3 6RB and Auckland, Melbourne, Singapore and Toronto.

ISBN 1-85532-650-7

Printed in Hong Kong
Page design Jenny Stewart

Contents

Minus its perspex registration plate, lost during an earlier encounter with an immovable object in the Derbyshire Dales (the editor's fault) a newly supplied 90 Defender rests beneath the church spire in the beautiful village of Chatsworth. The ubiquitous Land Rover is as much fun on road as off, its height and strength lending a feeling of security and of superiority over mere saloon car drivers

Foreword

As Manager of Land Rover's Presentations and Demonstrations department I am pleased to have been able to assist Chris Bennett with the compilation of this book. Having worked for Land Rover for over a quarter of a century I am naturally keen to read about, and look at, pictures of Land Rovers in a wide variety of settings.

Over the past few years environmentalists, quite rightly, have drawn attention to the many ways in which our environment can be damaged. Some people have pointed the finger at off-road vehicles – and that of course means Land Rovers.

As the creator of the world's most famous four wheel drive vehicles Land Rover is keen to lead the way in promoting sensitive use of the environment. After all, our customers represent a substantial proportion of the world's off-road drivers – people who are able to embrace our own policy of responsible driving.

We keenly urge all Land Rover owners to follow procedures, designed to safeguard the environment, which are laid down in our owners' handbooks and manuals. We want people to get the most out of their vehicles while at the same time enjoying the countryside.

As a matter of policy we continually urge people not to disturb the wildlife so it is important to bear in mind that animals should always take priority over our own progress when travelling off-road. We should be aware of the nervousness of animals and be prepared to switch off our engines and wait until they have moved on.

We condemn those who drive as if they are taking part in a motor sport rally. Powerful engines do not necessarily need high revs, and noise can also be a pollutant. The aim of the Land Rover driver should be to get from A to B as safely and in as much comfort as possible.

We have experience of driving in all sorts of conditions in all parts of the world whether it be in mountains or through water or in snow or deserts. Our guiding principle is to ensure that not only we, but our children and our children's children, can enjoy the landscapes and countryside that we have the pleasure to experience.

Roger Crathorne

In 1991 the Land Rover Driving Experience Centre was launched and, for the first time a facility at the Solihull-based factory became available to offer private purchasers the official word on off-road driving techniques. The team of instructors under the guidance of Roger Crathorne utilize the $4\frac{1}{2}$ miles of demanding tracks and obstacles, collectively known as the Jungle Track, to provide individual purchasers of vehicles with one-on-one tuition

Introduction

The Land Rover went into production in 1948 as a stop gap measure; this extraordinary vehicle has since become the product of a separate company, Europe's only dedicated volume four-wheel-drive manufacturer. The vehicles have traditionally been rugged and simple: Land Rover estimates that something like two-thirds of its entire production is still in use today. Unlike the affluent west, with next-day parts deliveries, diagnostic computers and skilled workshop staff, most countries where Land Rovers work for their living only have very primitive maintenance facilities, extremely poor roads and severe shortages of parts; yet somehow, these venerable workhorses continue to serve their communities.

The vehicle's unique structure makes it ideal for a wide variety of modifications. Land Rovers have parachuted, hovered, floated, been converted into half-tracks and even had their road wheels removed and replaced with toothed wheels driving four tracks, one for each wheel. This book is a pictorial celebration of one of the best loved and hardest driven vehicles ever produced.

A 110 Defender at Eastnor Castle, premier test centre for Land Rover. The Castle was built in 1812 during the Napoleonic Wars, as the country residence of the second Lord Somers, a construction job that commanded the then princely sum of £12,000. The grounds provide an ideal variety of terrain for off-road vehicle testing

A brief history

After the Second World War severe shortages continued for over a decade. In the later part of the Forties, sheet steel was still in desperately short supply and strictly rationed, with most going to those companies which were active in the export field. Rover, alas, had never been particularly interested in selling overseas and in order to keep its workforce going, it had to start exporting from scratch and was therefore confronted with a catch 22 situation: no export record, no steel, no steel, no exports.

Fortunately, the massive boom in aircraft production had led to huge aluminium stocks, and with the end of the war, the aircraft industry slowed down, leaving a considerable surplus. Aluminium is light, corrosion-resistant, fairly easy to work and quite expensive; but steel was simply not obtainable. This post-war supply situation paved the way for the world's most famous four-wheel-drive vehicle.

In 1947, The Rover Company realised that its pre-war models were not really suitable for export, so unless they came up with something else, the company was doomed. Maurice and Spencer Wilkes were the leading lights of the company. Maurice owned a farm in Anglesey where an ex-WD Jeep was in constant use. Spares were very hard to come by in the UK and this vehicle had seen wartime service. When Maurice looked around for an alternative, he found, to his considerable surprise, that nothing was available. Deciding that a market must exist for such a vehicle, he set about planning an agricultural car along the lines of the Willys Jeep but using the Rover P3 engine, gearbox and back axle. Scarce steel was only used for the chassis and front bulkhead, where the structural strength of

Built in 1949, this rare example of an early wood framed 80-in Estate Car forms part of the Dunsfold Land Rover Museum. One of only eight examples currently known to exist, she remains in an original and unrestored condition having been rescued from the clutches of a Leicestershire chicken farm in 1972. A four cylinder 1.6 litre petrol engine powers the vehicle which has a carrying capacity for seven people

THE ROVER Co Ltd
SOLIHULL
RECOMMENDED LUBRICANTS AGRICULTURAL GRADE

ENGINE		STEERING	GEARBOX & POWER TAKE-OFF	FRONT & REAR AXLE GEARS	STEERING RELAY LEVER BEARINGS	TRACTA' UNIVERSAL JOINTS	STEERING BALL JOINTS PROPELLER SHAFT SPLINE, HUBS & GREASE GUN NIPPLES
SUMMER	WINTER						
AGRICASTROL MED	AGRICASTROL LIGHT	AGRICASTROL GEAR OIL MED	AGRICASTROL HEAVY	AGRICASTROL GEAR OIL EP	AGRICASTROL GEAR OIL MED	AGRICASTROL GEAR OIL EP	AGRICASTROL GREASE HEAVY
ESSOLUBE 30	ESSOLUBE 20	ESSO GEAR OIL 90 MED	ESSOLUBE 50	ESSO EXPEE COMPOUND 90	ESSO GEAR OIL 90 MED	ESSO EXPEE COMPOUND 140	ESSO GREASE
PRICE'S OLYMPIA M	PRICE'S OLYMPIA F	PRICE'S OLYMPIA GEAR DK	PRICE'S OLYMPIA C	PRICE'S OLYMPIA EP	PRICE'S OLYMPIA GEAR DK	PRICE'S OLYMPIA EP	PRICE'S BELMOLINE C
SHELL TRACTOR OIL 30 SAE MED	SHELL TRACTOR OIL 20 SAE LIGHT	SHELL TRACTOR GEAR OIL SAE 140	SHELL TRACTOR OIL 50 SAE HEAVY	SHELL EP TRACTOR GEAR OIL 90 EP	SHELL TRACTOR GEAR OIL SAE 140	SHELL EP TRACTOR GEAR OIL 140 EP	SHELL TRACTOR GREASE
VACUUM TRACTOR OIL 630	VACUUM TRACTOR OIL 620	VACUUM TRACTOR GEAR OIL 140	VACUUM TRACTOR OIL 650	VACUUM TRACTOR EP GEAR OIL	VACUUM TRACTOR GEAR OIL 140	VACUUM TRACTOR EP GEAR OIL	VACUUM TRACTOR GREASE SOFT

this material was essential, and various body cappings to ensure body rigidity. The major panels were all Birmabright aluminium alloy.

Due to an overall lack of machinery and funds, the box section chassis was simply four welded pre-formed sheets of steel. This was, however, so successful that all short-wheel-base vehicles were built in the same manner right up to the introduction of the Land Rover 90 in 1984. The only truly new component was the transfer box giving high and low ratios. The existing Rover axle was used at both ends. The front axle was modified with swivel pins allowing the front wheels to steer.

A pre-production run of 48 vehicles was built in early 1948 in time for the launch at the Amsterdam Motor Show. Several of these vehicles still exist, but the unique centre steer prototype can only be found in photographic archives. Half of the pre-production vehicles were left-hand-drive, and one of the earliest of this batch that is known to have survived is R4 at the National Motor Museum at Beaulieu, although several others have been rescued and restored.

The original Land Rover had an 80-in wheelbase and was driven by a 1.6 litre side-valve engine. In keeping with the agricultural marketing strategy, this vehicle, which a decade later became known as the Series I, had power takeoff facilities at both ends and in the centre, so that belt driven machinery could be run independently. Tests of pre-production models not only included the normal endurance testing, economy runs and towing capabilities but also took ploughing performance into account.

Early press reports, road tests and engineers' reports were all glowing in their praise of this extraordinary little vehicle, but today's driver would raise his eyebrows at what he would have received in the way of creature comforts. Initially, everything was extra, including a spare wheel and canvas hood, although when series production started, these items became standard. A heater was an optional extra for many years.

In 1952 the engine was enlarged to two litres and in 1954 the wheelbase lengthened from 80in to 86in for greater power and better load space, thus silencing criticism from many quarters. For the bigger engine, the early, permanent four-wheel-drive system with freewheel overrun to the front wheels was changed in favour of 2/4-wheel-drive high ratio and 4 × 4 low ratio that continued right up to the early years of the 110, introduced

Detail of manufacturers plates fitted to a 1948 80-in chassis. The Land Rover was first introduced at the Amsterdam Motor Show on 30 April 1948, designed primarily to fulfil a need for a utility vehicle to accommodate the world agricultural and industrial markets

in 1983. At the same time as the short wheelbase model increased its length, the long wheelbase was born: the 107in.

The advent of the 107in was admission that the Land Rover was no longer seen as a stop-gap vehicle but rather as a model in its own right, and thus worthy of development.

Rover, in common with a lot of other companies, had absolutely no experience of diesel engines, but nevertheless set about developing a new generation diesel. At the same time, the company was working on a new petrol engine. The diesel had a capacity of 2,052cc and the petrol unit was the more familiar 2,286cc, better known as the $2\frac{1}{4}$ litre. The new petrol engine took a lot of the design elements from the diesel, ensuring that it was very rugged. The years have shown that this engine can withstand the most appalling abuse and somehow keep running.

In 1956 the wheelbase was increased again but this time by 2 inches in the engine bay. The following year the pieces fell into place with the introduction of the new diesel.

Ten years down the line, the Rover management team felt that the primitive styling of the Series I needed improvement. Times and the economy had changed, and while so too had the Land Rover, it still looked pretty basic. Thus the Series II was born and the rounded sides and overall style remains with us to this day. The flat, slab sides were made much more attractive and the additions of small skirts improved the proportions when viewed side-on and also screened the fuel tank.

Standing resplendent in the afternoon sun together with a rather more current vintage HS 125 executive jet, this one and a quarter ton Series IIB Forward Control vehicle dates from the late 1960s. This particular example, fitted with a Rover six cylinder 2.6 litre petrol engine saw service with the British Army, although similar vehicles were also used by the Royal Air Force and regular fire brigades. The vehicle's water capacity of 115 gallons was dispensed by an HCB-Angus 810 light fire appliance powered by a Coventry Climax pump

The next major change was the Series IIA. The diesel was bored out to the same capacity as the petrol engine along with the launch of a new model that again survives to this day; the twelve seater.

1962 also saw a much more dramatic vehicle appear. The Forward Control vehicle was effectively built upon a standard LWB chassis with the heavy duty axles mounted under rather than over the springs. The track grew by 4in and the wheelbase by 1in to help improve stability. This increased ground clearance and the additional subframe that carried the body, coupled to much bigger springs and tyres, made for a larger load bed and greater carrying capacity. In the mid 1960s, the six cylinder 2.6 litre engine from the P5 coupé was fitted to the FC and also found its way into the 12-seater station wagons.

By the end of the 1960s, many export markets were requesting that the headlamps should no longer nestle close together in the radiator grill, so they were moved out onto the wings. The interior had also been mildly facelifted and various improvements introduced covering basic instrumentation, ergonomics and wipers.

1970 heralded the arrival of the vehicle that is still the one to beat, after nearly 22 years. The coil sprung Range Rover was the first all terrain vehicle that actually had a saloon-like ride and a decent turn of speed; but it's a vehicle worthy of its own book, so it's not included in this one.

1971 saw the introduction of the Series III. There were very few noticeable changes to the outside of the vehicle except for a new, plastic radiator grill. This proved not to be popular in Australia where the old

Built in 1966 on chassis No. 1, VXC 100F was the prototype of a model known officially as the 110-in Bonneted Control Vehicle. Powered by a six cylinder, 3 litre engine with special five speed gearbox she was designed to meet the Ministry of Defence's requirement for an air-portable gun tractor. Unfortunately, at the completion of the trials the project was abandoned in favour of the 101-in Forward Control, this particular vehicle ending her working days at the factory with lawn mower towing duties

steel type had been extremely useful when suspended over a fire to cook steaks. Inside, the Series III boasted radically improved trim, ventilation and insulation as well as a new gearbox with synchromesh on all forward gears, (Series II and its variants only had synchro on third and fourth), better brakes and improved axles.

There was an acute shortage of cash throughout the 1970s which prevented the development of new models or variants. After more or less a decade bereft of development, the Land Rover story moved forward once more in 1979 with the advent of the Stage I V8. The radiator was moved forward flush with the headlamps and a new bonnet style was introduced. The engine, transmission and front axle were adapted from the Range Rover, but in order that people did not get too carried away in a vehicle that still featured drum brakes all round, restrictors were placed in the inlet manifold. At around the same era, the 'County' style appeared for the first time. Land Rovers could now boast such refinements as cloth seats and tinted glass along with body graphics informing the public that this Land Rover was a little bit special.

The last of the Series III saw the introduction of the High Capacity Pick Up, but in 1983, the all-new Land Rover 110 was unveiled. Featuring a wider track and a higher, single piece windscreen, the rest of the styling was pretty traditional apart from the wheel arch spats, but under the skin there were major changes. The four cylinder versions boasted five-speed gearboxes with either full-time or part-time four-wheel-drive, coil springing and a completely revised interior. The $2\frac{1}{4}$ petrol engine remained, but the diesel grew to $2\frac{1}{2}$ litres and the part-time four-wheel-drive option was dropped.

The 1984 launch of the 90 heralded the current style of Land Rovers. Right from the start, the 90 had wind-up windows, which were then

Also constructed around chassis No. 1, this is the prototype of the 88-in military lightweight used as trials vehicle by the MOD. Duly accepted and officially designated the $\frac{1}{2}$-ton air-portable FFR (Fitted For Radio) the 'lightweight' is fitted with a $2\frac{1}{4}$-litre, four-cylinder petrol engine and 24-volt system as opposed to standard civilian 12 volt. She was restored to her former glory in 1984 by the Dunsfold museum. The impressive collection, which now numbers over 40 vehicles, has expanded progressively since founder Brian Bashall acquired his first Land Rover. It includes many rare and historically important vehicles which, had it not been for the foresight of the Museum's founders, may well have been lost for all time

introduced onto the 110 and for the first time, a V8 was fitted to a SWB model. The combination of the evergreen 3.5 litre engine in a short vehicle with minimum overhangs (an improvement on the Series III as the suspension is more compact), has made the 90 the most effective production off-road vehicle available today.

Over the years, the advantages of an aluminium body that can be hosed down with no fear of rust has been recognised by the company and retained. Land Rovers also have the ability to tow 3.5 tonnes on a trailer with overrun brakes, or up to 4 tonnes with additional air brakes – a class best. In 1986 the $2\frac{1}{2}$ litre diesel gained a turbocharger which provided a welcome power boost.

The impact of the launch of the Discovery can be gauged by taking a look at sales figures in the relevant period in various markets: in the Middle East, for example, sales increased by 38% in the first nine months of 1991 against the same period in the previous year. The Iraqi invasion of Kuwait delayed the launch there, but after the Gulf War a special Land Rover task force organised the supply of vehicles to help in the reconstruction of the country. Not surprisingly, if you consider for a moment the devastation and the kind of work that standard Land Rovers and those from Special Vehicles are designed for, sales increased ten-fold post-war . . .

Featuring a $2\frac{1}{4}$-litre petrol engine together with four-speed box and optional two- or four-wheel-drive, this is chassis No. 1 of the renowned Ninety. Built in 1984, this original prototype actually featured a combination of modified 88-in body panels on a shortened 110-in chassis. Although this early pre-production vehicle featured an actual 90-in wheelbase this was in practice found to give a rather 'choppy' ride, so production vehicles were given a wheelbase of 92.9 inches

By the middle of 1988, the new Land Rover was an open secret, although its final form was yet to be seen. Either way, this new model, the Discovery, was to be only the third all-new vehicle since 1948 and the first for 19 years.

The 1980s saw the Japanese develop and exploit the market for comfortable, slightly benign looking off-road vehicles and they attacked the market in the huge gap between the utilitarian Land Rover and the luxurious Range Rover. It was a market that Land Rover decided to exploit. The Discovery was therefore launched in 1989. Built upon a proven chassis and drive train the vehicle used new production technology, ensuring better build quality than ever before. The real surprise was the new 200 Tdi diesel engine. A direct injection, intercooled turbo 2.5 litre four-cylinder engine, this unit won the heart of everyone who drove it, as did the overall performance of the new model.

With Land Rover now firmly a manufacturing brand name, model names were required for the three sectors, so, in 1990, the 90, 110 and 127 Land Rovers became Defenders. At the same time, the Tdi engine ousted the old $2\frac{1}{2}$ turbo unit and suddenly, Land Rover had a really outstanding diesel engine in the old workhorse.

Suitably kitted out the ubiquitous 110 County Defender permits the carrying of twelve occupants in real style. Long gone are the days when this was a purely utilitarian vehicle. Current variants included within the 90/110/130-in wheelbase specifications offer a high degree of comfort for both driver and passenger alike, whilst retaining all of its renowned off-road capabilities and load-carrying and towing potential

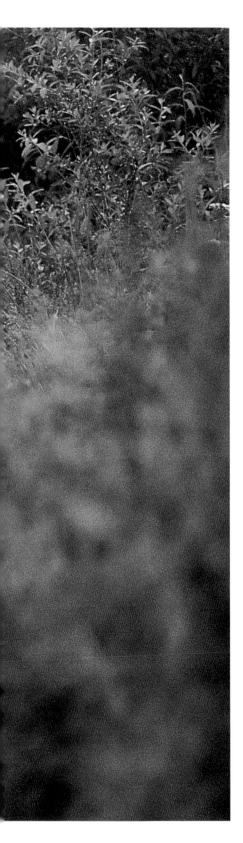

Left

A visitor to the facilities at David Bowyer's Off Road Centre in Devon, TMY 157 is probably one of the finest examples of an early 1948 Series I in existence. Nicknamed 'Tommy' with reference to its registration, this immaculate 80-in took owner Andrew Stevens, Chairman of the Land Rover Series One Club, a full seven years to restore

Above

The Defender, latest in a long line of pedigree vehicles. Launched at the beginning of 1991, this 110 is seen in the picturesque little Oxfordshire town of Burford. This particular vehicle is equipped with the new 2.5 Tdi turbocharged direct injection diesel engine, a highly efficient powerplant which offers many improvements over the previous naturally aspirated unit. Improvements such as a 25% increase in available power and torque whilst burning 25% less in fuel, allowing a major increase in top speed and acceleration for better fuel economy

Left

'Tommy' the 1948 Series I demonstrates that wheel articulation was pretty effective in the old days too. She is fitted with a mechanical, crankshaft-driven capstan winch used in practice by winding three turns of the 20mm synthetic fibre rope around the bollard to take the strain

Above

A fine example of an ex-military 101-in 1-ton Forward Control Land Rover, designed and built in the early 1970s to provide the military with a powerful vehicle capable of carrying and towing considerable loads. Powered by a standard 3.5 litre V8 the 101 had, in common with its smaller $\frac{1}{2}$-ton stable mate, many easily detachable parts designed to reduce its weight for the purposes of air-portability

Front-Line Land Rovers

Given that the inspiration of the Land Rover came from the jeep, the sales team must have always had its eye on the British Army. Initially, the post-war Army was on an efficiency drive and decided to rationalise major components. In the late 1940s and early 1950s, the Army was committed to buying the Austin Champ, but such were the delays to the programme, Land Rovers were bought as a stop-gap measure. After having used both vehicles side by side, it was clear that the Land Rover offered better value for money, all the more so when Armoured Personnel Carriers were replacing four-wheel-drive vehicles at the front.

The first thing a soldier does is to read the plate giving axle and towing weights. The second thing he does is to ignore it! Thus, the Land Rovers were given a beating, and that was before the specialists cast thoughtful eyes over the vehicle. During the war, the Long Range Desert Group had used a variety of vehicles for armed reconnaissance and naturally, in the light of this experience, wished to continue to develop such activities. The upshot of this was the development of the 109. First of all, the Army wanted a greater carrying capacity, so the springs, shackles and brakes were taken off the Series II Forward Control and fitted onto a standard 109, increasing its payload to 1 tonne. The SAS then worked their own particular magic on the vehicle for desert work and created the Pink Panthers. Pink is the best camouflage in the desert, and these vehicles were extremely heavily armed with two machine guns, radios, smoke and grenade launchers and a tank busting bazooka-type weapon, as well as long-range tanks, sand ladders and extra ammunition. The chances are that these vehicles were always operating at close to their maximum design weight.

The Army also decided that it wished to air lift Land Rovers. The Westland Wessex helicopter of the day had a carrying capacity of 2,500lbs,

This ungainly looking beast, shod in its Avon-manufactured inflatable air-bags, was the very first official vehicle in the Bashall collection. Acquired in 1966 she is officially designated as the One-Ton APGP Amphibian (Air Portable, General Purpose) built on a 109-in chassis. The military vehicle provided, in addition to air-portability, a minor amphibious capability, suitable for seaborne landings. This particular example dates from 1964 and is currently believed to be the only one still carrying its airbags. A small propeller mounted on the rear PTO (Power Take Off) provided water-borne propulsion whilst limited steering was achieved by use of the front wheels

rather less than the weight of an 88in, yet precision helicopter drops made a lot of operational sense. Attempts had been made to parachute vehicles, but the damage was such that the idea was shelved.

In order to cater for this particular need, Land Rover went to work on the body. It was impractical to reduce chassis and engine weight, both in terms of factory production and long-term durability in the field, so the engineers returned to the Series I look but made it even more basic, with no rounded edges at all. Items like doors, bonnet, hood and spare wheel were designed to be lifted off quickly and easily, but this still left the vehicle about 150lbs too heavy. Fortunately, the Army could live with this penalty and as time progressed, so more powerful helicopters were developed and this ceased to be a problem. A huge number of Series II & III lightweights were built and they are now flooding onto the civilian market as the Army re-equips with Defenders. The lightweight was never originally offered for open sale.

Apart from the Pink Panthers, the Army has put the Land Rover to a variety of uses, including ambulance, staff car and even evaluated it as a half track. Extra axles have been added, both driven and non-driven, while specialist builders have created armoured cars, security vans, vehicles designed to sweep a minefield as well as fitting a wide variety of accurate weaponry, particularly for the role of hit-and-run tank buster.

While the Series II FC never really caught on, the arrival of the V8 changed a lot of minds, especially when the Forward Control was re-worked. This time it was needed as a gun tractor, although as is usual with the British Army, other and varied uses were found for the vehicle.

The FC 101 had a wheelbase of 101in, but even with the powerful V8 was still light enough to be dangled under a helicopter and drag a gun about upon arrival. The FC 101 has been used as an ambulance, as well as for radio communications, various maintenance roles and for a lot of expedition work. The bulk of these units are soft tops, but every so often a hard top comes up for sale. The FC 101 was only ever built for the military, although as these vehicles are phased out, so the civilian market is snapping them up.

In June 1986 Land Rover unveiled a new forward control (meaning the cab is situated well forwards to maximise load carrying area) load carrying vehicle codenamed the 'Llama'. It featured a 110-in chassis fitted with the aluminium 3.5 litre V8 engine and was designed to provide a general purpose two-ton vehicle that could be adapted for use as a communications unit, personnel carrier or weapons platform. Unfortunately, the MOD didn't see the virtues of the Llama and the vehicle never saw production. This particular example, No. 2 of eight prototypes produced, was used for cold weather trials by Land Rover

One of the great beauties of the Land Rover bodywork for the military is that being aluminium, if the vehicle is damaged or mildly bent, then a good thump with a hammer will bend the dent more or less flat again and a dollop of paint completes the repair. A steel-bodied vehicle would have to be professionally repaired if rust was not to burst through quite quickly.

A pristine example of the General Service SAS $\frac{3}{4}$-ton Land Rover 'Pink Panther'. Utilizing a standard Series IIA 109-in chassis, Marshall's of Cambridge converted 72 vehicles during the late 1960s to fulfil a requirement by the Special Air Service Regiment for a long range desert/patrol vehicle. Under normal army use these veritable gunships were painted in standard olive drab but, for desert operations a more suitable pink finish was provided; hence the nickname. The vehicle bristles with military hardware: two 7.62mm General Purpose Machine Guns (GPMG), two 7.62mm Self Loading Rifles (SLR), three compartment grenade holders, four sets of triple smoke dischargers, a signal pistol and, last but very definitely not least, a Carl Gustav rocket launcher. Navigational equipment includes magnetic compass, sun compass and theodolite together with two radios. Two auxiliary forty-gallon fuel tanks provided endurance for extended remote vehicle operations. Of the 72 originally built, over twenty are still known to survive, being sold out of service in the mid 1980s and replaced by an updated vehicle built around the 110

Designed as an armoured patrol vehicle for light defence duties and border work, this vehicle was built around a strengthened Series III one ton, 109-in chassis. Designed as a cost effective means of combating urban or rural terrorist operations, these vehicles, which have been sold to 72 different countries, left the factory as a chassis cab, the armoured bodywork being built by Shorland of Belfast. This particular armoured car saw extensive service in Northern Ireland with the Ulster Defence Regiment

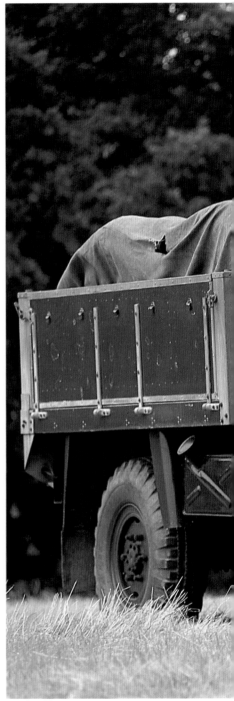

Brian Bashall, Land Rover enthusiast, founder member of the All Wheel Drive Club of Great Britain and hard working curator of the Dunsfold Collection lends a little scale to 'Lofty', the Museum's nickname for this oversized, 129-in experimental load-carrying vehicle. Developed primarily with military application in mind, Lofty was fitted with an experimental $2\frac{1}{2}$-litre turbocharged diesel engine but sadly, pitted against the Mercedes-Benz Unimog, it was never put into production. The Museum's vehicle, the fifth of five built, dates from 1964, purchased for the collection five years later

Above
An orderly parade of smart brand new Defenders await imminent deployment to their military owners

Right
An agreement was reached in 1956 between the then Rover Company and Metalurgica de Santa Ana of Spain resulting in the production of licence-built vehicles bearing the name Santana. The 109-in Series III vehicle featured here is a 1978 vintage example developed for the Spanish military. Powered by a $3\frac{1}{2}$-litre six-cylinder petrol engine this particular vehicle was used by Land Rover for evaluation purposes

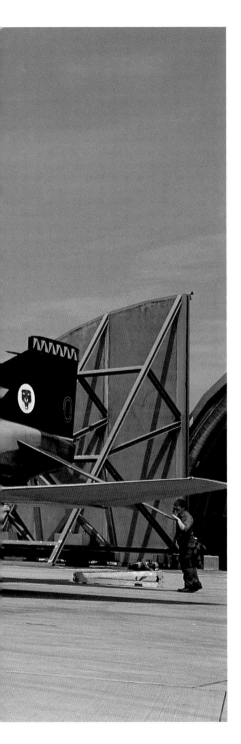

Left
A standard military Series III as owned and operated by the Royal Air Force poses on the hard stand together with McDonnell Douglas Phantom FGR2, belonging to No 74(F) Squadron at RAF Wattisham in Suffolk

Above
A common, all military establishment Series III lightweight, this example equipped with trailer and spotlights

Left

The next generation, this military 90 accompanies a somewhat older vintage Victor Tanker. Christened Sweet Sue this Victor was operated to good effect during the Gulf War by the crews of No 55 Squadron stationed at RAF Marham in Norfolk

Above

These majestic and beautiful looking jets which were originally built as bombers and later converted to air-refuelling operations are sadly starting to feel their age. This Victor, which was due to transit to the United States experienced a minor engine fire necessitating prompt action by Marham's efficient emergency crews. A 110 Defender ambulance attends the busy scene but, thankfully, its services were not required

Variations on a theme

The simple construction of the Land Rover has encouraged people to produce some extraordinary vehicles. The Land Rover has been turned into a hovercraft, giant lawn mower, aircraft loading ramp, fire engine, ambulance and a lot more besides. Special Projects was set up exclusively to handle enquiries for modifications to the vehicles and Special Vehicle Operations, (SVO) continues that tradition to this day. SVO created a lot of demand for the 127in wheelbase vehicle. Initially, a 110 was taken off the line, stripped, cut in half and lengthened. The 127in, known these days as the Defender 130, has its own production line and SVO can either supply a custom-built vehicle to a customer's requirements or simply a chassis cab for completion elsewhere.

The great simplicity of construction ensures that modifications are relatively easy. Add to this simple bodywork one of the most robust chassis in the business, and the flexibility of the Land Rover is clear.

A number of six-wheel-drive 110 vehicles have been built and adapted for use as high-rise platforms. The electricity generating companies use a variety of 110 and 130 hard top and crew cab models to maintain the high voltage power lines. The same type of SVO vehicles have been exported to Kuwait for the reconstruction after the Gulf War.

Another area where the Land Rover was pressed into service was on the railways. Initially, the wheels were dished out to match the gauge of the lines, but in order to gain traction, solid rubber tyres were shrunk onto

Chris 'Buster' Bashall (left), together with Dave Rowlands attend to some minor on-site mods necessary prior to this Land/Range Rover hybrid taking to the mud again. Christened 'The Mule' for obvious reasons the vehicle, based on a Range Rover chassis with Land Rover body, boasts ample power, supplied by an ex-Jensen Interceptor 6.3-litre Chrysler engine, capable of a meaty 370bhp...

the railway style wheels. This was all well and good until the driver braked a little too hard and locked up a wheel, at which point a flat spot was created which in turn led to unacceptable vibrations. A better scheme was to widen the track but retain the normal road wheels with a simple bogie front and back to locate the vehicle on the tracks. The advantage here was that the Land Rover could be driven on the road in the normal way, as well as running up and down rails. It could also be turned around rather than having to reverse for maybe several miles, an activity for which the gearbox was never designed. At the Discovery launch, this device was resurrected for a press call which was somewhat startling. It is not every day that one sees a fully liveried police car towing five standard British Rail carriages, a total weight of over 170 tonnes!

The Cuthbertson conversion was an equally intriguing idea, although few survive. Created with a view to traversing very soft and boggy ground, the conversion was a sub frame with a miniature caterpillar track at each corner. The Land Rover was dropped onto the frame, the wheels replaced with toothed cogs and a track wrapped round this drive wheel and the two wheels on the frame, producing a triangular track configuration at each corner. The front wheels steered in the normal way, so the vehicle drove exactly like a car. The whole thing stood a long way off the ground and getting in and out cannot have been easy. A further refinement was added whereby a large air bag was fitted at each end giving buoyancy, whereby the vehicle became aquatic.

When Vickers was developing the first large hovercraft, it hit upon the idea of using a Land Rover coupled to an air cushion for crop spraying. Due to very low ground pressure, damage would be minimal while steering and braking would be retained, with the added advantage that the whole rig could be driven on the public highway.

Land Rovers have long proved popular as small, highly mobile fire appliances. Carmichael extended the wheelbase of the Range Rover and increased its payload by adding a non-driven axle. Considerable numbers

... a 370bhp that Dave Rowlands was grateful for as, sitting squat and bulldog like on its massive Yokohama Mud Digger tyres, the Mule prepares to take up the strain and propel Dave's Eagle Jeep out of the mire

of these machines were purchased by the RAF and civilian airfields with the express role of being the first vehicle onto a crash scene, ready to spray the aircraft with foam. These vehicles could not carry a lot of foam, but there was sufficient to start work until the bigger hardware arrived.

In August 1991, Land Rover launched its range of fast response, specially adapted paramedic models based on the Discovery. SVO stretched the wheelbase to 116 inches to make room for all the necessary equipment including a full length trolley stretcher. It goes without saying that the vehicle made light work of off-road terrain and the steepest motorway embankments.

Apart from the factory, many outside companies offer a huge variety of modifications and equipment, from roll bars to roof racks, jerry cans to winches. Several companies modify vehicles very extensively: the Land Rover Hi-Roof was in fact developed by an outside specialist, EV Engineering of Waterlooville. There are many companies offering a huge range of equipment for any activity that a customer wishes to pursue, from recreational green-laning to crossing the Sahara, from Road Taxed Vehicle Trials to high-performance Competitive Safari vehicles.

Mission accomplished, the Mule powers off to create a splash elsewhere. Chris Bashall is owner of Surrey Off Road Specialists, capable of rebuilding your vehicle to just about any spec you care to mention and, as far as Buster's concerned, the more outrageous the better

Above
A product of Land Rover's Special Vehicle Operations (SVO) division, this brand-new ambulance conversion features the 127-in wheelbase, officially referred to as the 130, one of many SVO 130 chassis variations

Right
Equipped with winch and Michelin XCL mud-plugging tyres, an SVO product, the 130 Crew Cab Box Body negotiates the 42% side slope on the factory's Land Track, part of the famous Jungle Track at Solihull

The Camel Trophy

The Camel Trophy is a unique institution, which is why it has lasted so long, and in Europe, is every bit as well known and indeed in certain countries is more enthusiastically followed than the Paris Dakar Raid.

Unlike the Paris Dakar, or indeed any other Rally or Raid, places on the Camel Trophy are not for sale. Places are hard won on sheer ability alone and the selection process is hard graft, both mentally and physically and those who make the grade are very exceptional people.

The Trophy itself is not a race, but rather the ultimate off-road adventure. The term 'off-road' is used in the loosest sense in that the road is not sealed. All the routes chosen exist, although they might not have been used for years or even decades. Equally, training concentrates on the fact that the environment and needs of local people must be respected. The convoy is entirely self-sufficient in everything apart from water and fuel. As well as the competitors vehicles, there are vehicles carrying spares, journalists, an ambulance and a communications vehicle. The convoy has a doctor present all the time and every Cameleer has to have a reasonable command of English.

The Camel Trophy has often meant much more time spent repairing roads and bridges than actually travelling, while the doctor can often be found treating local inhabitants en route. Generally held in hot and humid parts of the world, those from the temperate climes find the going particularly arduous, especially when falling behind schedule results in the luxuries of life going by the board – sleeping and eating, for example.

Every model of Land Rover has been used on the Camel Trophy at some point and many from several Trophies ago are still performing sterling service in national and international selections. Every other branch of international motor sport, if one can put the Camel Trophy under that heading, has massive budgets, often running into seven figures. This is

Colin Parkes, one of Land Rover's highly experienced driving instructors, advises a candidate for the '91 Camel Trophy during the British selections at Eastnor. The annual Camel Trophy expedition has been described as the 'last great adventure' and certainly, those who dream of challenging, both physically and emotionally, some of the world's most gruelling and hostile terrain need look no further. Camel Trophy is three long, hard weeks of man and machine pitted against some of the most arduous territory the globe has to offer; from the Taiga Forest in Siberia to the swamps of Sulawesi and the steamy rain forests of the Amazon

spent on weird, hybrid cars that bear no resemblance at all to what is sold in the showroom, yet Land Rover has shown, year after year, that the more or less standard product is good enough for one of the most gruelling events in the world.

Any modification is conducted in-house using standard parts from within the Land Rover range of vehicles. Thus, the Discoverys used in Russia and Tanzania/Burundi featured heavy duty rear differentials and half shafts from another Land Rover model, either a 90 or 110. Apart from that, the preparation is a matter of additions rather than modifications. The engine, transmission, drive train and suspension are completely standard, although, doubtless, the engines will be adjusted to run on poorer quality fuel where appropriate and such advice would form part of Land Rover's service to those who wish to use the product in really harsh climates with poor resources.

As for the rest, most of the parts would either be available from the parts department of any Land Rover dealer or from specialist firms that handle certain items on behalf of Land Rover. Thus, the roll cage and under body protection is provided by a factory approved subcontractor, while additional lighting, bull bars, winch, roof rack and so forth can all be ordered through the local dealer.

Above
Famous badge in its element

Right
Having successfully constructed their log bridge, Louise Temperley one of the two female candidates in the '91 selections, jubilantly guides her partner over the obstacle. The selection trials, which will eventually cut the 24 hopefuls down to national team pairings, are extremely demanding in their own right. All candidates are expected to live in simulated expedition conditions, camping under canvas irrespective of the weather and, at any time during the day or night may be called upon to perform exhausting tasks to their instructor's satisfaction. Such tasks are designed to observe competitors' fitness, endurance, initiative and spirit, qualities that will prove absolutely essential on the Trophy expedition

As in any competitive event, there has to be a winner, but there are various different awards apart from the Camel Trophy itself. Team spirit is one of the most coveted, and this is decided by the crews and awarded to the team who have contributed most to keeping the convoy moving, both physically and morally. The Trophy itself is decided by special tasks set along the route, but any participant is quick to point out that, unlike just about any other modern competition, it really is the taking part that counts.

Camel Trophy is now a brand name in its own right and markets a collection of watches, clothing, luggage and footwear, a business that the company already estimates as being worth some $300 million a year.

Although they have supplied the vehicles throughout the Camel expedition's history, Land Rover were not official sponsors until 1992. The gruelling 1600-km Guyana event includes five major river crossings (with no bridges, of course). The 16 two-man teams drive 16 Discoverys, with 21 assorted Defenders and Discoverys in support.

A Land Rover, of course, is not unbreakable – nothing is. And if something snaps, as the Camel Trophy organiser, Iain Chapman, said with a wolfish grin, 'This is where you discover who your friends are, because they may have to tow you maybe 1,000 kilometres through the jungle!'

Bob Ives kicks up the mud as he demonstrates driving technique, Trophy style. The Camel Trophy was originated in 1980 in what was then West Germany. Using identically kitted vehicles, three teams, all from Germany drove 1000 miles of the Transamazonica Highway in Brazil, a two-week feat of endurance battling against the heat and mud of the Amazon Jungle. This first expedition was such a success that it became an annual event. The 1991 Camel saw the largest participation yet, 17 countries fighting their way for 18 days from Dar es Salaam in Tanzania to Burundi. Worldwide interest in the Camel Trophy is intense, nearly two million people applying to participate in the event each year

Above
Brothers Bob and Joe Ives, winners of the 1989 Camel Trophy expedition to the Amazon take on the fiendishly demanding terrain of Eastnor Castle as they demonstrate winching techniques, in spectacular fashion, utilizing a 45-degree incline for the purpose

Right
The Brothers Ives crack the February ice in preparation for a (very cold) water task during the selections.

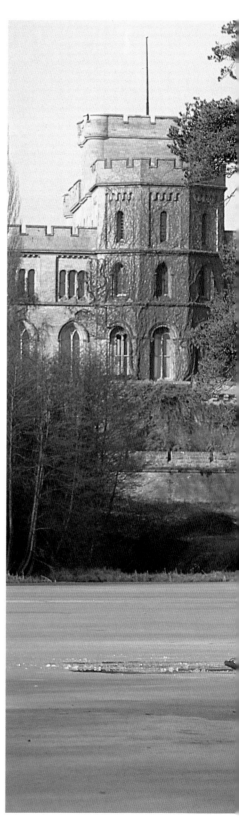

At the completion of another day's
Camel training Dennis Patstone
prepares his charge for tomorrow's
endeavours. With the exception of
the very first expedition, Land Rover
vehicles in various combinations have
been used exclusively on the Trophy.
The 1991 expedition to East Africa
involved a total of 36 vehicles, the
twenty three Discoverys supported by
thirteen 110 Defenders.

Originally the winners of the coveted Trophy were the team judged to have given the most outstanding performance during the event. However, as the scale of the expedition grew so this method of adjudication became more impractical. In consequence the teams are now judged during performance of 'Special Tasks'. These tasks, held at the beginning and end of the event proper are designed to simulate the kind of obstacles and terrain encountered during the actual Camel Trophy. Each task is designed to test physical endurance, mental agility, navigational and driving skills. A further award titled the 'Team Spirit' is given to the team observed to have made the strongest contribution to the event and to have displayed the most outstanding Trophy spirit and attitude. Voted for and selected by the participating team members themselves this award is, in many ways, more prized than the Camel Trophy itself

Now retired to the more genteel life of public relations work and training, an ex-Camel 90 exhibits many hard won battle scars. Vehicles used during the Trophy are, to all intents and purposes as standard, although there are of course certain modifications that are essential for expedition use. An external roll cage incorporating roof rack is one such addition, rollovers being a common and, in some instances highly spectacular occurrence on the Trophy. Bull bars, raised air intakes and a powerful electric winch are also essential pieces of basic kit. Other less essential but important extras include underside guards and spot lamps, together with a myriad loose articles such as hi-lift jack, ropes, pulley, snatch blocks and extra fuel, water and provisions

Above

The '91 British selection team and hopefuls gather for a photo call together with ex-Trophy vehicles. Turkey were to excel during the Tanzania–Burundi event, the team of Menderes Utku and Bulent Ozler walking away with both the Camel Trophy and Team Spirit award. Britain's pairing of Timothy Dray and Andrew Street gained a commendable fifth place

Right

A Guyana '92 Trophy pre-scout 110 lifts an XCL during some rather attention-grabbing winch operations, aided by members of the local population. Almost immediately one Camel Trophy expedition has been completed the organising team under Event Manager Iain Chapman, an ex-Camel participant, have to start thinking about where the next will be. Decisions for primary and secondary locations are made, advance scout teams visiting the selected areas surveying routes, obtaining necessary diplomatic clearances and permissions and organising the logistical requirements

A mud-spattered Duncan Barbour feeds cable back onto the Husky Superwinch's drum, taking care to avoid pinching or kinking the wire, both of which could seriously undermine the cable's breaking strain with potentially dangerous results

Above

For Sale ... Ex Camel Trophy expedition vehicle, one careful owner, never raced or rallied. A support 110 freshly returned from the Tanzania–Burundi '91 Camel Trophy exhibits a few hard-earned battle scars acquired during its epic journey. There aren't many vehicles that would still be capable of driving after collecting this sort of heavy duty damage; but, for the reliable Land Rover it's a walk in the park

Right

For 1992 the Camel Trophy returns to its traditional South American roots, transiting north from the city of Manaus in Brazil along the Transamazonica Highway, crossing the Rio Branco River and Guyanese Border. From here on the intrepid convoy follows existing but long-lost tracks through thick forest and across grassland savanna. Timed to coincide with the rainy season the rugged terrain combined with sizeable rivers and dense jungle provide a worthy challenge to vehicles and participants

Your Land Rover

With the three model line-up of Range Rover, Discovery and Defender, Land Rover Ltd has a powerful market presence in all but the bottom end of the recreational market which remains the domain of the Japanese and latterly, Vauxhall. The Defender is the Land Rover that more regularly works hard for its living, both in this country and overseas. In many parts of the world, the first car a human being ever sees is a Land Rover.

There are five British magazines dedicated to the four wheel drive scene and one, *Land Rover Owner*, that only deals with Solihull's finest. There are over seventy clubs in the UK, the biggest single block of which is the Association of Rover Clubs, the ruling body for the official Land Rover clubs. Overseas, there are Land Rover clubs aplenty.

Land Rover has always rigidly resisted any attempts to compromise the off-road performance of its products. It was only in the 1991 model year, for example, that roll bars were finally fitted to the Range Rover as standard. These devices have restricted overall wheel travel by just a few millimetres, but the change was very carefully considered.

Given that there is a Land Rover vehicle for every budget, the possibilities are endless. For those who live in rural areas, the vehicles can cope with just about anything that the weather can throw up, while going on a motoring holiday takes on a whole new meaning.

Regardless of whether you are the owner of a brand new, top model Range Rover or a second (or even umpteenth) hand Series II, it is important to learn the basics of off-tarmac driving, both in terms of technique and also where you can and cannot legally drive. There are a number of schools in the UK which specialise in off-road training and a

Sometimes when off-road, discretion is the better part of valour; especially when confronted by big muddy holes in the track. Larry Byrne, Northamptonshire Rights of Way Officer for the All Wheel Drive Club, prepares to manoeuvre his tried and tested 90 out of its sticky predicament. In situations when loss of traction is a possibility, always ensure that the differential lock is engaged in good time and prior to negotiating any potentially hazardous terrain, utilizing low-range gear selections suitable for the conditions ahead

good course should cover theory, vehicle preparation and basic kit, then move onto hands-on training. Some courses extend training to winching, self-recovery and even go into the really rough side of life, demonstrating how to build log bridges and how to fry eggs in a brake drum! The first off-road training school was created by David Bowyer in Devon and since then, David has formed and is chairman of TORTA, The Off Road Training Association, the aim of which is to establish a minimum standard of instruction in this field.

The importance of basic training cannot be over-emphasised. Such is the competence of the Land Rover range, a lot of drivers can overcome various obstacles without ever knowing how or why, but there will come the day when familiarity, coupled to ignorance, will result in copious tears being shed. These courses are designed to permit novices to begin to explore the capabilities of their vehicles and to carefully consider how they are likely to be used in the future and thus what additional equipment is desirable.

Most clubs will have a Right of Way Officer whose job is to keep abreast of route re-classifications as well as advising members which lanes are becoming damaged and need a rest. He will equally be able to advise which lanes are becoming overgrown and need to be used! Green laning is a very pleasant way to spend a day, but it is up to everyone involved to ensure that the law is obeyed and common sense codes observed.

Apart from advising about rights of way, the various clubs organise competitive events ranging from Road Taxed Vehicle Trials (RTVT) through to Comp Safaris which are contested by custom-built vehicles. The former cost very little, with entry fees generally being around the £10–£15 mark. Vehicles require little in the way of preparation beyond an additional throttle closing spring on four-cylinder petrol engines and a proper towing/recovery point on the back, and for preference, one on the front as well. Beyond that, the vehicle must be in a proper state of maintenance and repair, something required for highway use anyway. If

David Bowyer, director of his own off-road driving school in Devon monitors the ensuing events as 'GBH', his loyal 90 prepares to receive a helping tug from a 110, utilizing a kinetic energy recovery rope for the purpose. Such ropes, in addition to obvious strength, possess an elastic property. When the towing vehicle powers forward under moderate throttle the rope initially stretches storing up kinetic energy before moments later contracting, thereby applying a smooth but extremely powerful recovering force to the stricken vehicle. But such ropes obviously demand the most stringent safety precautions

competing under the Association of Rover Clubs (ARC) rules, the vehicle must be original. The ARC yearbook has full details of the rules and club officials can keep competitors abreast of any changes.

Comp Safaris are rather more exciting to watch but participation involves some further investment, although this is still one of the cheapest forms of motor sport around. The vehicles tend to be quite specialised, often running V6 Ford or V8 Rover engines in either Series I or II vehicles or on coil-sprung Range Rover chassis with most of the body removed save for a roll cage. These vehicles have often been shortened as well as having had all excess overhang removed. Being specialised and high-performance, with the vehicles often taking off, crash helmets are obligatory.

Clubs also hold regular rallies, treasure hunts and meets where every sort of issue and problem is aired and discussed. The ARC National Rally, hosted by a different member club every year, is one of the high spots of a keen Land Rover owner's year. Apart from visitors from all over the country, overseas club members also appear in large numbers. Visitors at the 1991 event in Plymouth came from all over Germany, France, Belgium, Holland and Denmark.

Club membership is also a rich source of technical information, spares and knowledge about which of the local garages really know their business when it comes to Land Rovers. The most expensive is not necessarily the best. Details of local clubs will be found in the 4WD magazines.

Left
Whether nimbly picking its way over a rock-strewn surface, hauling its way through the mud, wading through rivers or cruising down the King's Road, the Land Rover conquers all obstacles

Far left
With the 110 Defender as much at home in these surroundings as on snow or sand, a small convoy of vehicles 'tread lightly' as they navigate a track bracketed by a thick pine forest. Loose spacing of vehicles is important for safety reasons, the zoom lens used for this picture condensing perspective, making the convoy appear tighter than it actually was

Above
Purely for the camera's benefit Larry Byrne, a veteran of many demanding off-road sorties takes his 90 County Station Wagon from the path. Prior to negotiating any green lanes it's most important to confirm legal right of way for motor vehicles

Left
Four is the ideal number of participants in a convoy of this nature, additions causing potential problems in communications and convoy management

Far right

Even the masters of the art get bogged on occasion, but what counts is how safely and efficiently the situation is remedied. In this instance David Bowyer, to the interest of all concerned makes full use of his equipment to extract his vehicle from its muddy entrapment. Employing the vehicle-mounted Husky winch David performs a clean extraction, mindful of avoiding damage to his natural surroundings. Winching may seem aggressive but, in the hands of the knowledgeable it actually minimizes damage to the soft muddy tracks; a technique of driving into the trouble area and then taking to the cable being ideal, avoiding unnecessary wheelspin and pulling the vehicle slowly but smoothly out rather than digging deeply in. The All Wheel Drive Club have taken a commendable and responsible approach to green laning, tasking work parties to repair and maintain lanes for the continued future use of both vehicles and pedestrians alike, in addition to voluntarily restricting use of especially stricken areas until a full restoration has been undertaken

Above

Clive Ritchie is at the helm of the 90 soft-top GBH as it negotiates a minor decline, cautiously selecting a path to avoid large, protruding rocks that may damage the vehicle's axle differentials. GBH is equipped with a 3.5 Efi V8 engine providing ample power for even the most extreme off-road situations

Above

Fitted with immensely strong protective bull bar, Larry Byrne's County 90 manoeuvres along the rock-strewn ancient drovers track, The Gap in the Brecons. Most off-road driving is conducted at slow speed, limiting potential damage to both vehicle and scenery; the dictum 'as slow as possible but as fast as necessary' is carefully followed

Right

Still looking remarkably clean in its smart red and white paint the '91 spec 110 traverses a valley track part way along the Gap Road

David Bowyer eases GBH over the brow into an extremely steep and rocky descent at a location along the Gap known as Blown Bridge. For obvious reasons, such extreme terrain requires a full knowledge of vehicle handling and driving technique and it is very wise to view the track ahead on foot prior to negotiating on four wheels. Descending a slope such as this (always in first gear low range for maximum engine braking) it's possible that the vehicle's own weight may initiate a slide, the first sign of which is an increase in vehicle speed without a coincidental increase in engine rpm. In order to recover the situation with some degree of dignity the throttle must be opened just enough to increase wheel speed to match descent speed. The use of the foot brake, however instinctive, must be avoided at all costs as this could readily cause a complete loss of control

A 110 County Defender winds along a characteristically picturesque little Welsh track, one of the many rarely used drovers tracks that weave a patchwork through that part of the country

Above

*The 90 soft-top crawls along at a
snails pace as Clive Ritchie attempts
to minimise potential damage to
vehicle and tyres on the rocky terrain
which is particularly unforgiving.
'GBH' spends much of her life off-
road for, when not negotiating tracks
in deepest Wales she's up to her sills
in mud at David Bowyer's Off-Road
Centre*

Right

*Larry Byrne ascends the verge to
avoid a large rock in his path*

Left
Wet and dirty enthusiasts have fun on private ground as, seated in his modified Series I an over-zealous off-roader gets a rearward tug...

Above
... once extracted he happily attempts an alternative route

Left

At this stage still looking resplendent in its smart green and white paint job H935 EWK a Tdi 90, traverses a mildly bumpy track in Derbyshire. For the purpose of this photograph its spare wheel has been moved onto the bonnet mounting in contrast to the more usual tailgate position. The Tdi-equipped 90 returns an efficient 32 miles per gallon at 56mph, which provides a considerable saving in fuel over the less economic 3.5 litre V8 petrol engine. In comparison with earlier diesel engines it has more than sufficient power and is most pleasant to drive

Above

Suitably attired for some serious wet and muddy work and his Series I fitted with a roll cage, this Welsh mud plugger enjoys life as he monitors his counterparts' attempts at a particularly glutinous obstacle

The Tdi 90 climbs effortlessly up a steep grassy incline with Osprey's intrepid automotive editor in (and then out of) the driving seat. All Defender models can, under normal load and tractive conditions, surmount a 45-degree or 1-in-1 incline which is normally enough to grab the driver's attention. Steep grassy slopes such as this should be treated with the utmost care and respect particularly when damp; the greasy surface can be extremely treacherous

Above
*A Series III soft top paddles around
the mud tracks, simply in its element*

Right
*After a couple of days mud plugging
the 90 may not look quite so clean
but, in the author's opinion, it does
look rather more interesting*

Left

The Right Honourable Roland Lytton of Minehead, Somerset, plows his much modified vehicle through the muddy sand of the Ministry of Defence's ranges at Long Valley during an AWDC event. Whilst at first glance this vehicle may appear fairly standard, it is in fact highly modified, being a Land/Range Rover hybrid fitted with a six-cylinder, 3-litre Ford engine. Standard issue for this kind of work are a strong bull bar and front-mounted tow bracket

Above

Many events that the AWDC operate are advertised as non-damaging and suitable for those who may wish to get a little muddy without the potential risk of serious damage to their pride and joy. The owner of this V8-fitted Series II is obviously rather more concerned that his vehicle isn't quite dirty enough yet, but it certainly won't stay that way for long!

*This characterful mid '50s Series I,
more ancient than its occupants, is
getting back to nature in the wilds
of Aldershot*

Another AWDC competition safari vehicle, this time an ex-military Series III lightweight owned by Glyn Barge of Winchester. Glyn's vehicle also boasts a robust exterior roll cage, an important and very wise accessory for the serious off-road vehicle

'Thunderbox', John Haythorne's 80-in Series 1 of 1953 vintage which he rescued some years ago from a boat yard on the River Crouch in Essex. John employs his faithful old Thunderbox for both everyday road use and also as a recovery vehicle during AWDC events. The Series 1 covers about 10,000 miles each year

*With the wind in their hair an
intrepid duo tackle a non-damaging
trials section in their Series III*

Based on an 86-in Series I, Maurice Planders' left-hand-drive competition safari vehicle packs a punch, mated with a Rover V8 engine enabling it to hop along somewhat more rapidly than its original specification would have quoted

Left
Glyn Barge's lightweight takes to the
air as he negotiates a rather tight
left-hander at speed

Above
An apparently more or less off-the-
shelf Series III truck cab reveals a
little more about its owners
adventurous intentions courtesy of the
beefy roll bar

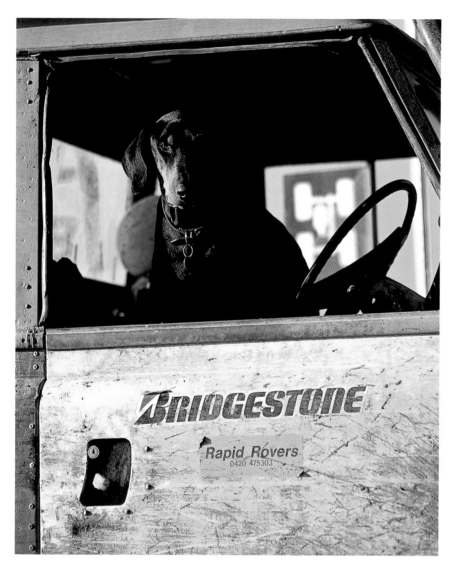

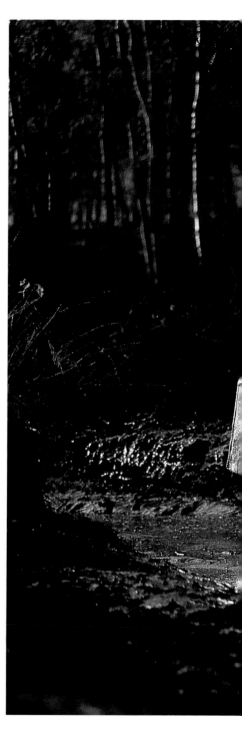

Above
A man's best friends; his Rover and his dog

Right
The afternoon sun reflects off the watery mud as a Series III long wheelbase cruises round

Martin Ing of Oxted in Surrey takes full advantage of the prevailing snowy conditions to enjoy the airy virtues of his top-less Rover. Martin's vehicle, a 1964 vintage Series IIA spent much of its working life on a Wiltshire Farm, prior to retirement to RV (Recreational Vehicle) duties a couple of years ago. Top off, screen down and wind in the hair

Tom Wallis, manager of High Ridge
Farm at Merle Common in Surrey
braves the winter scenery to attend to
his flock. In these severe conditions
the Land Rover comes into its own,
enabling life to go on more or less as
normal, while the less fortunate slip
and slide in the icy trap

Owner of High Ridge, 'gentleman farmer' Dr Keith Day stands proudly in front of his 110 County with faithful Holly in attendance

Larry Byrne cautiously navigates the log bridge spanning a wide ditch, deep in the seclusion of a Devonshire wood

Left
Clive Ritchie utilizes the electric Huskie Superwinch fitted to his vehicle to haul it bodily through a sticky combination of mud and foliage...

Above
... and then feeds the wire cable back onto the drum, the use of thick leather gloves preventing the possibility of a nasty cut from any stray, razor-sharp metal strands

Above
Massively strong bull bars such as this smart example by ARB incorporating a Warn winch can perform an outstanding job at preventing front-end damage. Care must be taken however, to avoid mounting a bar which protrudes unduly which will restrict the vehicle's approach angle in extreme off-road conditions

Right
Emerging from the depths of thick woodland the 101 Forward Control exhibits massive ground clearance partly provided by its large tyres

Above
Valve is mated with rim of a Michelin XCL destined for military use

Left
At this intermediate stage resembling some kind of giant Meccano set, a convoy of Defender body panels progress along the 'Cricket Pitch', en route for the paint shop. Nearly three-quarters of the vehicles produced by Land Rover are exported, an achievement that merited the Queen's Award for Export in 1990. It is Land Rover's proud boast that there are only two countries in the entire world – North Vietnam and Albania – that have to date been immune to the efforts of their entrepreneurial sales force

Left
Spot the famous trade mark on this XCL's tread; a tough tyre for a tough vehicle

Right
At the Solihull based factory complex, employees get down to the specialist task of fabricating and welding door frames. In contrast to many other modern car manufacturers where computer controlled robots have stripped much of the human element out of the production process, most of Land Rover's construction is still done by hand. This permits their employees to become rather more involved in the product than would otherwise be the case and, in addition gives cause for both pride and enthusiasm towards the company and its vehicles

Above
Freshly cast steel connecting rods await machining and finishing prior to their final assembly, together with the myriad other components that combine to make . . .

... a V8 engine. The 3.5 litre (eight
cylinder) V8 petrol engine provides a
power output of 134 bhp at 5,000
rpm, giving more than sufficient
torque for off-road conditions

Nearing completion, brand-new Defenders creep down the assembly line. Just about the only thing that is predictable about their future working life is that it will be long

Left

A Demonstration Team 110 emerges from the Jungle Track at Solihull. The Jungle Track simulates many of the features and extreme conditions likely to be encountered off-road around the world. Deeply rutted muddy tracks, deep water wading areas, unnervingly steep gradients and side slopes are just a few of the features purposefully built in. It's easy to forget that you are still within the confines of Land Rover's 270-acre Solihull plant when the imagination says you're in the Amazon on the Camel Trophy!

Above

A new looking Defender 110 negotiates the wheel articulation bumps situated on the factory's Land Track, demonstrating the benefits and flexibility of its coil suspension, permitting all four wheels to remain in contact with the ground and under power whilst heavily cross axled

Above

With inevitable white-knuckle journalist at the helm, a 110 rushes up from one of Eastnor's many muddy rock tracks

Right

Fresh off the muddy tracks a 110 Defender Truck Cab at Eastnor Castle. The Castle, which lies amidst the Malvern Hills in Herefordshire, has maintained a close working relationship with Land Rover for many years. The Castle's ample, scenic grounds provide over 100km of challenging and varied tracks, and are regularly used for vehicle testing and development together with customer demonstrations

Above

Working together as a team, Roger Crathorne together with colleague John Carter, manager of the Driving Experience Centre, sort out a small problem with their winch following some (very) heavy duty operations at Eastnor. Roger who first joined Land Rover in 1964, has been heading demonstrations and presentations for the past fourteen years

Left

Roger Crathorne, Land Rover's Presentations and Demonstrations Manager patiently oversees operations as Sue Baker, correspondent for the Observer newspaper gets hands-on experience of winch operations. Eastnor frequently provides facilities for media and press days

A 110 is frozen in motion by fill flash